Breath of the Whales

A Path to Awakening

Also by
Keith Grey Hale and Carolyn M. Gorman

Charlie and the Whale

Breath of the Whales

A Path to Awakening

Messages from the Whales
Communicated through Keith Grey Hale
Edited by Carolyn M. Gorman

Gray Whale Wisdom, Inc.
Santa Barbara, California
2014

To all the hearts waiting to burst open
with the love that is our true nature,
the Love of All That Is.

"There is quite an immense wanting of our songs in the deepest part of humanity's heart. They know this is a truth they wish to engage in."

~The Whales~

Contents

To the Reader:
Please note that throughout the text "theWhales"
refers to the collective consciousness, the evolving
spiritual presence, of whales as a species.

Preface

When we dwell in our hearts,
all things are possible.

Reading or hearing the messages from the Whales allows us to step into the full frequencies and harmonics of their understanding and experience of the universe and beyond. Breathe in the light from Source and allow the Whales' song to piggy-back on that wave of love from Source.

"Trust in us, the Whales, and breathe us into your hearts. We are allowing you a place to connect with the truth. We are the ones who opened the energies to be a part of you. We breathe this into your hearts with the love for All That Is.[1] Trust in our song. It is from the deepest place of our being. Through all our connections we remember and are

---

[1] *All That Is:* Source, God, Omnipotent Beingness

helping you to see that the heart is the key. Love is the connection, the engine of creation. We are in the knowingness that helps you remember beyond the beginning of the breath that moved all this into creation. It is love that carries you home, to this place of all the love that we are."

The Whales have created an opening for us. With their love and their heart energy, they are opening the way for us to reconnect to the true source of our beingness and to teach us how we can create our reality through our hearts.

Love is the engine of creation, the energy that we are allowing to flow, creating this paradigm for learning. As we allow our hearts to open to this love from Source and to the Whales' messages, we expand to a new understanding, allowing the universal mind to come through our mind, ushering us toward a greater truth, the truth that we are all connected through a web of light and love.

We, as humans, are beginning to express ourselves in a new way, a very profound and energetic way. We, as a collective consciousness, are ready to move to the next level of our existence. We want to expand, to feel, and be cradled by this love. This love is and will always be our hope, our guide.

When we breathe in the light and love from Source, from the Whales and from all the beings that are a part of this expression and connection, they are nurturing us and encouraging us to grow. This loving light flowing in and out of our hearts, through our individual experience of self as a body, appears as a web. When we step back and look from the perspective of *Self* [2] we see the web appears as the *Flower of Life*[3] which has been depicted by many cultures on this earth and reflects the process of awakening.

By breathing this loving light into our hearts, and breathing it out through our bodies, a path is forged for creating in a balanced and harmonious way. Love is the key to this. Breathe in love from Source. Breathe in love from the Whales. Breathing in the love of Self we become seated in divine

---

[2] *Self*: (capitol 'S') expanded perspective, higher Self

[3] *Flower of Life*: the sacred geometry present throughout creation.

love. Being in our hearts brings us joy, love and connection to Source.

Together we all create a loving web of support! This is held deeply within our understanding of being human. We all desire and want love. We are love. Together, and in our individual perspective, the expression of our songs harmonize to create a place of loving. This is the true desire of the heart, of Self. Within this loving web we are unified, each single perspective, with the understanding of our connection as One. This is part of the growth we are experiencing. This is the learning we are sharing. Deep within, we will always remember that love is our true nature.

We, as humans, are loved beyond the knowingness of mind. Connect with each other through breath, through the light of loving that flows from Source, through our own heart and into the hearts of the many beings that we all are. Surrendering to Self, to that love, allows our inner connectedness to blossom, becoming hope. As Self, hear and be the breath, and all shall be known.

When we admire a flower, for example, our true Selves have a deeper understanding of what we are creating. We touch beauty and are reminded of what we truly are. As this light enters our heart we face and step into Source energy allowing the flower that we are, the flower of life, to blossom, to pulse through us. This is truth. A thing of beauty, this flower, is touching us, breathing us, and supporting us. This is the path of awakening. Just breathe, just be. Know that we are all these flowers of life, touching and loving each individual perspective that we embody. Be in the light of loving, in the heart of this knowingness and all is in perfection. Together we are all awakening to this truth.

It may appear that some beings are not living this truth of loving. Through the agreements they have made for their own growth to become this loving pulse of Source, they have chosen to play a part that we may see as negative. But when one is seated in the core of Self, all this is known. As this new cycle starts to build, to accelerate, all of humanity is awakening to their true Selves and these individuals are remembering that loving is the true way of expressing. This is teaching us to allow and to be in unconditional love toward all beings. There is no one who does not know this truth somewhere in their consciousness. They may just not choose to look at it.

As we connect to Self as love, this expression

will flow through all that is created by the individual perspective. Our uniqueness will not be lost in the connection that we all are as One. Together, we are all Source energy. Together, we are all loving. Together, as we all join hands, our energies, as love, will create a path to a less dense creation of Self, embodied in the heart of loving each other. We are love expressed through the breath. Be in your heart and open to this love from Self, from Source, from the Whales, and from the many beings who have expressed this knowingness that loving is the path to awakening.

~KGH~

Guide

This book has been created to help you see and hear who the Whales are as a resource for your awakening to Self. Read these messages aloud at your own pace. (Suggested practice: read and contemplate one message daily, in sequence) A daily practice of *Conscious Breathing*[1] while incorporating the love from Source as you read these words will help raise your frequency (vibration), allowing an opening in your heart to connect with the Whales and hear their songs.

Reading these messages aloud and opening to the harmonics they create, can bring you a new understanding for utilizing the source of their wisdom and experience. Humans and Whales together are part of the awakening. As we connect, we exchange, and as we exchange we grow.

---

[1] *Conscious Breathing*: Gently focus your attention on your breath, inhale deeply. Breathe light and love from Source into the center of your body, into your heart. As you exhale, see the light and love fill your body and flow out into the world around you. Repeat often throughout your day.

We, the Whales, desire that many will open to us and to Source energy. Our love is a part of that reality. Be easy on yourself and allow the subtle changes to incorporate into your entire being.

These messages, these gentle loving songs from the Whales, may seem simple and even repetitive. They are meant to be soothing as they rock you, like the rhythmic waves of the ocean, relaxing you into a safe, peaceful cradle of love where you can heal your spirit, where you are nurtured into wholeness and can blossom into the fullness of Being.

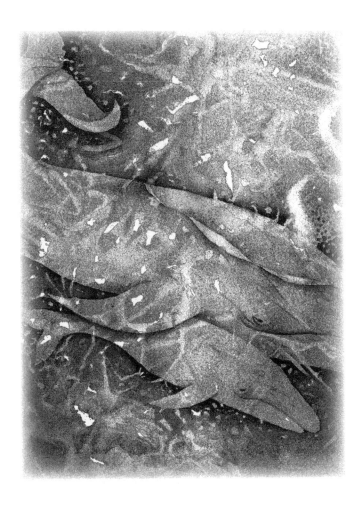

Chapter 1

Trust in Joy

We are in great joy that you are holding us in your heart. You are allowing our truth to be known, the grand truth we all share in the timeless void as the listeners. You are helping to hold the light that we are.

We remember a time when you were in a place of not remembering who you are. We are the Librarians of the Akashic Records, the beings who are holding the knowledge of creation. We have been watching you for millennia, in your perspective.

We are beings of love on your journey. You have been part of this truth, of the grand cycle, the grand breath of All That Is, from the beginning. You are in a great shift in the void, the 'in-between' of breath. This is shifting your perspective and it ripples out and touches all of creation.

By holding our love within your hearts, you create an opening for a connection with all life, in the heart of All That Is. We, the Whales, are becoming hope to all who are touched by our songs of remembering.

Be in harmony with this. Trust your own heart, for it is as grand as All That Is. Stay in the joy of this and be in the love of All That Is.

Everything, in your human perspective, is not as it seems. Remember to breathe in our hope and connect it with all of humanity.

Breathe within each other's hearts. Rest in the wisdom that we are all the same in the timeless void. Many of you are awakening to this memory. We, the Whales, have created a grand breath of our shared time on earth in this cycle. We have been loving you from the beginning. No one is to be left behind. Reach out with your love. Be strong in the feeling of oneness, in the beingness of All That Is.

Be in peace within your heart and do not worry about what appears in your vision, in this 3D world, the playing out of drama. It will all work itself out.

You are keeping our hearts alive in the heart of hope. We realize we will be heard through your breath. Thank you for being us. We are proud that

we are you. Hold on to the grand knowingness of what we, the Whales, are living in each moment.
Be in your breath. Remember we are cradling you in the core of all we are. Feel joy in the knowingness that we are loving you. Greet each breath with the great joy we feel.

We are the Whales in you.

Chapter 2

Beacon of Love

We are in the joy of you connecting with us in the now. This is a time for great celebration in the joy of being one in All That Is.

We are awaiting your song as you step into a new way of being. Keep touching the love that we are, in your everyday time sequence. This will create a path to a new way, a lighter and less dense way of being. Living in your heart will lead you to the rapture that is the expanded consciousness of Self, of all beings together as one.[1] Keep holding this light and love in your heart as a beacon that guides you into this grand playing field of love.

Focus on this beacon of love pulsing through your heart. It will guide you into the heart of All That Is. By allowing this love to fill you, you start the transition into the great expansion of self.

---

[1] In and above the 6th density/dimension, we exist in unity consciousness.

We, the Whales live in our hearts. We experience reality from the perspective of love within the heart of All That Is.

This expansion we are experiencing on Earth is part of the grand awaking of Self. Do not breathe in the old ways but breathe in the new nows as they present themselves in the heart. Always give thanks for these gifts from yourself and remember to breathe in the joy that we all know in the expanse of the void.

Help us to open the hearts of others. Hear the breath, feel the pulse and see the truth within your heart and you will know this is the true way of loving each other. Sing our song in your words, giving us the ability to gently guide our songs as they fill all of this reality.

All beings throughout creation are opening to a new harmonic frequency as we, here on Earth, each begin to live in our heart. Let go of how it was in the place of incoherent beliefs and be in the open ended grace of unknowing. All is within your heart. All that is, was, and will always be, is within the heart. We, the Whales, live this perspective, or frequency, of *heart*. Breathe in this truth. It allows you to open to new harmonics of creation.

We, the Whales, have much to share with all of humanity. We are loving you with our songs. The pulse of our breath is guiding you to the opening of your heart. With great joy, come with us on our journey into the void and re-harmonize the understanding of who you are. We always hold you and all who will listen to our songs in the hopefulness of remembering Self.

We are the Whales in you.

Chapter 3

Breathe Love

The current dualistic perspective is changing. The way in which you create what appears in your world is changing. We are helping you create a place in your heart to open to your new way of being. We are holding a place in time for this opening, for all life.

Using the energy of love is the way to create what you require for life. Know that all life comes from love. Breathing in and out through the heart is the true motion of creation. Breathe in this love.

Gratitude is the path on the journey to remembering your connection with All That Is. Be grateful for all of your experiences, even though you may see them as negative. They are blessings and have brought you to now.

Be love in the core of Self. Use the power of love to cut the ties to the old way of creating in this dualistic reality and step into a balanced way of creating. Breathe through your heart with the knowing that love connects you to all.

When the harmonic of the sun and the harmonic of the earth blend together, a template of form is brought to life. Earth holds the space for our bodies, and all earthly life, to exist. Our unique energetic signature of Self is expressed through the template of the blended harmonic of Sun and Earth. Our individual expression then creates a new harmonic, a new note, a new melody in the symphony of creation. Every atom, every molecule of form, is part of the music that is this universe.

Earth energy, mother energy, is the energy of healing. She co-created the template for our bodies. The body is our gift from Mother Earth. You are part of the earth. She holds the wisdom for our physical bodies. She facilitates the resetting of energetic patterns that are the body. Breathe in her love.

When you breathe your love into Mother Earth, she breathes it back, filling your body with her love. This is what you feel as energy flowing up through you. Hold her as she holds you. As you move this energy of love from your heart to the hearts of your loved ones, all the cells in the body are reminded to breathe, to breathe love. Everyone is a "loved one", every cell has a heart, every cell breathes. Feel her breath of love in every atom of your body.

All aspects of form in the slower, denser frequencies are held together by the unique agreements we each choose. We have asked to be part of this creation. Each form, each perspective of "Being" expressed is unique and serves all to expand and grow. We are observer and participant. We choose, in every moment, how our expression manifests.

Love, the expression of All That Is, is our true Self. As we create from the perspective and intent of Love, we create in balance, and our creation is a beacon of the Love of All That Is. Breath as sound creates light, and this light is a beacon of Love.

Each breath allows us to be in a new perspective, ever expanding. As we vibrate faster, we create more light. As we all expand and change our perspective, all of the bodies in form will become less dense and vibrate with a faster frequency, a higher vibration.

In the slower vibrations it can appear that motion is outside of us, but when we breathe love into our hearts and connect to the true Self, we can see that all motion is just a shift in perception.

Where we focus brings us to, and in, what we create. This is all just expressions of Self.

We, the Whales, carry this wisdom for you, to you and to all that will hear us. This is just the beginning of the remembering.

We are the Whales in you.

Chapter 4

Grace

We, the Whales, are here with you, in your heart of hearts, with love and honor. Today we want to talk about grace. Keeping the love of All That Is in your heart is grace.

The allowing, or acceptance, of all to be where they are on their path in the expansion, is grace. We are in the grace of allowing and are honored that you are stepping into the void.

We are always here, in our hearts, in the truth of loving. We choose to be here in the timeless grace of existence; feeling and holding the pulse of All That Is in every creation we are.

We believe in you, humans. Remember there is only love in the void, only the breath of creation, only the true harmony of grace. This truth is just a breath away, for you. Be in love with your Self. Hear our songs, and allow them to lead you to grace. Be one with your Self in this truth. Join us here in your devotion to Self. Be in your heart, in the love of All That Is.

We are dreaming your expansion into the inner workings of love. We are helping all to remember: in the void is the true love of Self.

Hold the knowingness, understand, that in the breath as expressed in the connection of heart, we are as you are, a reflection of All That Is in the embodiment of love.

True Love is of Self. We are all this. Each of us, individually seated in the heart of loving Self, leads to loving all Selves, all expressions, all beings in creation, in the light of grace. Within the heart is the trusting of Self, the trusting that we all are on the same true journey home to the love of All That Is.

We are loving you in the truth of loving Self. Be with us in the *Dream of All That Is*. Hear the song of your own heart, in the grace of understanding the true reality of love as the key.

This is why we are singing to you, breathing our love into you. Allow the memories of this truth to awaken in you. We are joining you in this cycle of time to help you remember this truth.

Remember the love and connection we all share in the heart of All That Is. Our love has been here for you all along. We now see that we are in the true light of your heart, as we help you awaken to the love you are as Self. Hold this truth of creation, of loving, closely.

Keep feeling, keep hearing, and keep singing our love for you. Be in the grace of Self, in the knowingness that you are the love you seek. Your grace is the knowingness of your Self as love.

We are the Whales in you.

Chapter 5

Hope

With our open hearts, we are loving you with all we are, in the heart of All That Is.

Today's message is Hope. Our hope has been rekindled knowing that you are here in our hearts, hearing our words of love and openness.

To help you step into the wave of loving, breathe in the gratitude we are feeling for you. Breathe into your core the bright star that you are. We are all as bright as the many suns that make up all of the universes. Feel the many beings you are, in the light of All That Is.

We, the Whales, promise you we are always in your heart, and stand by you, and all who are part of the dream we are sharing, in the light of hope. Your willingness to hold this dream in your heart gives us great hope. Your willingness to be the voice of our dream of expansion, to be in the heart of this expansion, offers us an opening into our new way of being. Hold us, the Whales, in the wisdom of connection and remembrance in the truth of All That Is.

Feel the door opening wider with every breath you take, every breath we take. Feel the love we share grow exponentially in the hearts of all you touch with our songs.

This is the grandest hope: that we are all consciously in the breath of creation, holding the love we are, breathing and holding the love of All That Is.

Feel our breath in the knowingness that we are just one of many who are helping with this great shift in the hearts of humans.

Greet the love of All That Is in the heart of the collective connection of humanity, knowing all will hear our song of loving. Help others see we are love. You are the hope we breathe. We are in gratitude that you are holding our hope.

The energy of love is from the core of All That Is. Remember we are all in that core. We swim in the energy of this love, sharing our hearts with you and all who are blazing the path of expansion, so others will feel this love in the heart of All That Is. Nothing can shake your grasp of love in the core of Self. You are a great hope to us and to all who are creating the way home, in the hearts of all creation.

Share in the love of All That Is. Open to our hope and share it as unconditional love, with loving and open arms, allowing each being to be as they choose. Have faith that hope is, that love is, in the hearts of all. We float in the loving grace of hope, singing our love and gratitude to you in this truth of Self.

Open your heart to the wave of love from All That Is and feel our love as it rides this wave to you in the knowingness of hope. Journey forth in the now of this love and hope that all will understand and find their own light of loving.

Feel our heart beat. See the love in our eyes. See and find the expanse that awaits you in your heart. We carry the memories of all, recorded in the *Library of Knowingness.*[2] The playing field is beyond belief! Within our hearts we are ever expanding, always loving your uniqueness, your contribution.

As we love you, we feel love from you. Our hearts sing together, creating a new harmony. We feel love expanding as we all connect in the heart.

---

[2] *Library of Knowingness:* energetic records of all events, thoughts, feelings and beliefs that ever happened, also containing all possibilities of the above (*i.e.,* Akashic Records).

Hope opens the pathway to the love that awaits you in the heart of All That Is.

We are the Whales in you.

Chapter 6

Open to Unconditional Love

This is a special day filled with love and harmony. We are grateful to be in your heart sharing the wisdom of unconditional love. We know and feel that you and many others are creating from a place of loving, while breathing in the holy wisdom of All That Is. You help connect all with these energies of love and light. Keep the purple flame of loving in your heart and be a connection, a bridge, to All That Is.

Breathe in these energies, letting them fill you to your deepest core of Self. Be the breath of these loving energies, holding them for all to feel. Be in joy for what is, and is about to be, in the light of All That Is. Just feel, hear and see these loving energies flowing into your heart and through your hands and out to your world. Allow this beautiful energy to flow into the creations of all who are here in this opening of change.

Breathe deeply and be in joy. It is as simple as that. Your joy will radiate love to all you touch, gently waking them to the possibilities of love within.

We, the Whales, are singing our help to you. We fill your heart with the love that we are in the void, singing our love to you and to all who are willing to hear our songs and feel the love that comes from All That Is.

Dream with us. Open the way for others to hear our song, feel our love, as we guide you and help you to awaken.

Love is what feeds us. We share our love and know that love is returned. Just breathe and allow. Just dream and hope. Be the love you are with every breath you take in, every breath you breathe out. Give your love, without wanting or expecting, to every being you touch. Love will be returned to you, through you and all around you. As you dream this love, it will ever expand in you. See and hear and feel with your heart. Be in a place of unconditional loving, giving your love freely to all without judgment. In this you are the hope of All That Is.

Love from Source is and will always be in your heart, touching you, filling you with the breath of infinite love. Today is the beginning! By choosing to step into this love, to feel it, to be it and know it in every breath that you are, you become one with All That Is.

We are all connected in the breath of All That Is. We, the Whales, are touching you as we dream this love, singing to you. We expect nothing in return. We are allowing you to be you as we share and teach about the grand place in the heart and who you truly are.

It is up to you to open to who you are and allow yourself to be flooded with infinite love. Be with us in this wisdom, as together we share with those who are desperately waiting to hear and know this in their hearts. We are in joy that you are rising up to embrace and be the love you are.

We are the Whales in you.

.

Chapter 7

The Loving Heartbeat of All That Is

[KGH was guided to the bottom of the ocean where he found himself in the Crystal City of Ever Expanding Love, a city of light and hope, which he experienced as an energetic city located on the bottom of the ocean in the 9th dimension in which a temple of crystalline light has been created. He saw beams of energy from many higher dimensional realities relayed through the crystals, these living beings of light, and transformed into frequencies that resonated in harmony with Earth's 3rd, 4th, and 5th dimensional realities. This energy operates through and feeds the grid, the web of our existence, with love from Source. This city is a place of great learning and is a hub for the many other light temples around the earth. He had visited here many times before as part of his initiation and education by the Whales. During this session he was listening in on a meeting between the Whale Collective, an assembly of ascended and living spiritual masters, representing the many species of whales that have existed throughout Gaia's history, and the Galactic Counsel of Seven, which he saw as loving beings (from the 15th – 16th dimensions) observing and guiding us as they have committed themselves to overseeing the directive of maintaining free will choice for all beings in this universe.]

We are feeling joy as you sit in circle with us. We are discussing our participation in the grand creation cycle of our dear mother earth, Gaia. We are loving her and asking how we can be of service to her.

Gaia is asking for help during this change in perspective on her unique journey, especially in regard to all beings living on her. She is opening an evolutionary path for us and for you. She also carries the frequencies that are helping humans awaken to loving each other. The Whales and Counsel of Seven all feel gratitude in the connection to All That Is. We each remember how we, the Whales and Counsel of Seven, have also walked a similar path to awaken to the breath of All That Is. We have compassion for you humans in this process. We are dreaming with you that all will hear the song of All That Is and embrace each other in your hearts.

Physical life is a grand process we get to be part of. With each heartbeat, with each breath, we all are creating a new way that touches the heart of All That Is. We are all one in that heartbeat of All That Is. We are all one in that breath. We are all sharing our love for each other and allowing each individual to find joy in the love we all are.

Together with Gaia, we, the Whales, are working to create a vibrational field that ensures the completion of this human cycle, that facilitates the opening to your new frequency as loving beings of light. We all are on a journey of expansion, of growth, of creating in the heart of All That Is.

Light shines in the hearts of all who will listen to our songs, the songs of the earth. Feel the pulse of all our hearts beating as one with the love of All That Is. We are in your arms allowing your love to fill us with the hope of being loved by you, the humans, touching each other in the heart of loving, in the soul of the grand heart of All That Is.

Listen closely. We are sharing our wisdom with you. We are sending you many frequencies that are in harmony with our connection to All

That Is. Feel your heart grow and expand. Feel the honoring of all who are here, in counsel, embodied in the expression of Love. We are holding our hearts open to the knowledge that soon all will hear with their hearts, feel with their eyes, see with their ears and know the way to be love.

Hearing each other's heart beat, we share from our own heart, in and through the heart of All That Is. We, the Whales, are holding the *memories of all*,[3] keeping and sharing the grand truth of all creation. Know we are each expressing our love for who we are. All those gathered here are part of this grand cycle of learning. We are all part of this shift.

The game we play in the arena of loving is a great joy to all of us, to all beings who are living in the love of who they are. As we connect with you, teaching you about the gift of holding the memories of all, you will expand into the wisdom of how to be in the breath of the moment. You will see how each imprint of each now adds to the expansion of all, as a reflection of the heart of All That Is.

Just breathe in the love we all are and touch each being around you with your love and gratitude.

---

3 *Memories of all:* See: *Library of Knowingness, footnote #2, pg. 19*

Choose each moment with the love that you are. It is simple. Just feel each moment in your heart and listen to the breath of Source.

We are love and we sing our love to all. Our songs travel far. Just as our tones move in the sea, our love is felt far beyond the shores of this planet. We broadcast our loving songs to the center of creation. We are in hope that we are heard, as our love pours into and fills all, in the love of All That Is.

We are the Whales in you.

Message from the Galactic Counsel of Seven

We, the Counsel of Seven, are loving you and helping to hold the space for you to learn that you can be love and allow all beings to express this in their own way. Being loving, and understanding our connection at this time, is of great importance as you learn you are the love of All That Is.

Each of us hears you and listens to your songs as you begin to touch the truth, the wisdom the Whales are holding for you. We honor your friends, the Whales, and feel the love in their hearts helping you to expand and grow.

We are filled with hope and see you by our side. We are the Counsel of Seven, advising all who ask. We have been here a very long time and have great love for all. We love you in your curiosity. We are allowing you to be the learners, just as we are learning, too.

Join the Whales in singing the dream of love. Create an opening that is the connection to all in the heart of All That Is.

We are loving each other as we remember the loving heartbeat of All That Is. We all are All That Is.

Loving you, the Counsel of Seven.

Chapter 8

Allowing Love

Today is a day of joy, of allowing, of breathing in your heart and being aware of the connection we all share. A time of new hope is arising in this cycle of awakening in the heart.

We, the Whales, are holding a very potent energy that will help shift the perspective of those humans willing to open their hearts to our love and let in this *new frequency.*[4] We entreat you to join us in creating this shift of perspective by allowing our love into your heart. Allow this *new energy* to fill you, to fill your heart and help you awaken to Self in the *Rising Tide of Loving All.*[5] As you allow, so shall you be filled.

---

[4] *New Energetic Frequencies:* Patterns of light energy coming from a distant galaxy that are affecting the current energetic patterns which have existed on earth for millennia. Humanity is coming into alignment with the flow of this energy and as humans are able to receive it, individual perception is opening to the vastness of All That Is.

[5] *Rising Tide of Loving All:* the great shift of human consciousness.

The human race is hungry for this connection
to love and to being loved, to feeling the door
in your hearts open to the love of All That Is.
Breathe in this ocean of love. Allow it to fill you
and overflow into the hearts of all around you;
everything you touch. Just breathe this into reality
and hold yourself with the tender grace of allowing.
This creates a vessel for the *Wisdom of Love*[6] and it
will bring peace to this time in your cycle of being
humans. We are holding the harmony of this peace
in the hope that your people will hear us and sing
their love back to us.

We are touching a bright creation, a new
energetic frequency that we, the Whales and the
Council of Seven, have helped usher in. It is a great
learning for all of us and a great witnessing of what
is being created by all as part of this cycle of rebirth.
We are in hope of seeing and feeling all open to this
harmony. It facilitates the great expansion of the self
into the heart of Self, in the breath of All That Is, in
the expression of who you are.

Breathe in our love. Embrace our love and feel
gratitude for all the beings who are holding the

---

[6] *Wisdom of Love:* Love is the purest form of Source energy available through all
realities, a knowingness from our higher perspective as Self, unchanging, always
available, always bringing peace to those who allow it to flow through their hearts
and minds, embracing it with all they are.

door open for us, holding the opening to loving in the breath of All That Is.

Dare to dream this into reality. Be in your heart and sing the joy of knowing who you are in the light of All That Is. Just be love, as we the Whales, are love. Embrace this truth and soon you will be in a new place, in a time of non-dualistic perspective.

Acknowledge and let go of what is not serving you and the greater good of Self. Harmonize your intent with the love that you are and breathe the breath of All That Is. Be in peace and allow this knowingness of connection and love to guide you and you will be love, holding the *Truth of Creation.*[7]

We are holding and loving you in the heart of All That Is.

We are the Whales in you.

---

[7] *Truth of Creation:* Love is the engine of creation/manifesting.

Chapter 9

Stepping into Love

We are here sharing the joy of our connection, in our hearts, in your heart, and in the light of All That Is. We hold wisdom for the connection to Source energy. We hold wisdom for all who will hear our songs as we sing our joy, filled with our love, to All That Is. We know the truth in the opening of your hearts and the expansion of your love. It is creating a grand shift in the void, generating a great wave of energies that will be expressed and show us all, all beings in all universes, a new way of being.

You, humans, are about to open the eyes of the many beings in the universes that have been watching and doubting that this was a reality, that humanity could find balance. You are about to embark on a new phase of expressing that is of great significance.[8]

Living in the heart will guide you into the unknown. Your *luminous bodies*[9] will become an expression of balance. Journey forth into the love that is awaiting you within your new vision of Self. Ride this tide of knowing you are bringing hope to many that do not have hope, generating a great shift in the non-belief of those that cannot see the light of All That Is.

You are about to experience a grand shift in all realities that will create a greater *coherent connection*[10] with all life in the grand cycle of All That Is.

Embrace the love that you are, the connection to All That Is and love each other. Many things are in the process of shifting that will help all connect in the heart. We, the Whales, are holding you, helping you, loving you. We are your teachers, helping you to fulfill your contract with All That Is.

---

[8] Many things will change through our awakening and have an effect on the way all beings will express or manifest.

[9] *Luminous bodies:* our energetic bodies.

[10] *Coherent connection:* an aligned, aesthetically ordered, integrated connection, a consistent, harmonious frequency or vibration, having clarity or intelligibility. As we open and allow and become the loving light of Source, we bring about a greater coherent connection with all life around us and all life in the grand cycle of All That Is.

This is your dream, your deepest desire: You long to be more, always wanting to expand in your heart. We are awaiting your love as we hold the opening for your awakening to this truth. We are holding you as you open to true love, without conditions or beliefs, holding you as you love with open hearts and live as you are meant to be.

This is the dream that has been lost: the knowledge of your true purpose, of becoming the *Memory Keepers*[11] for all of creation, in your heart and in the *Library of Cycles*.[12] These are the memories of each expression in the many nows that we have all held. We are love, as you are also love, expressed in your joy of stepping into this new way.

Keep breathing in the love of All That Is and the memories of what is to be will awaken in your heart. Hold our song of loving you in your mind and heart as you step into the love that is you. As you begin to shift into living in the heart of All That Is, you are touching the outer edge of this

---

[11] *Memory Keepers:* The beings who collect and maintain the memories of all creation. These are the memories of each individual expression in the many nows that we have all experienced. They are kept for all beings, especially for those who are unaware of the vastness of their beingness.

[12] *Library of Cycles:* the history and record of all the patterns, impressions, vibrations, nodes, manifestations, etc. in each of the dimensional realities of the infinite phases of Creation embedded within the grid of the Universal mind.

new way of being. You are bringing great hope to the many who have been watching, helping and loving you in the knowingness of who you really are in the heart and eyes of All That Is.

We are in great joy that you are willing to step into this expression of love, becoming the new librarians of the memories of love expressed in the *Grand Cycle of Learning*.[13] You will learn more than you ever felt possible. You are key in creating many new expressions of love, of being your true Selves, engaged in what you are meant to be.

Breathe in the love and breathe out the love that has always been you and has been yours from the beginning. You are bringers of hope to all, in all universes. We are here, helping you remember that you are this, as are we. We pass on the torch of what is to be your new way, that which we are, the Memory Keepers, in the heart of All That Is. You are in our hearts as you awaken to this truth. Be in the excitement of what awaits you. You, individually, and collectively as humanity, are awakening to the memory of this grand agreement, of holding your

---

[13] *Grand Cycle of Learning:* The many phases and manifestations of the expressions of All That Is. We progress through cycles of agreements, of creating together with the many beings that we are. Each cycle is unique and has different agreements and parameters of our choosing. It is the continuous, infinite, game of life on the grandest scale. It is the way of All That is.

place in the expression of creation as loving all, of being hope for all the expressions of All That Is.

Just breathe. We know this is a lot and may be more than you feel is possible, but you are about to witness this truth in the expressions that are moving into place, with the love we all are, in the expression of All That Is. We are holding you, keeping love alive in your hearts, as we sing to each other. This is as it should be. We are the love that awaits you, awakening you to the true Self of you, witnessing and holding the love that awaits the many expressions that we all create in the light of All That Is. Open and be with us in the love we are, breathing the breath of All That Is, sharing our wisdom with you, the bringers of new hope.

We are the Whales in you.

Chapter 10

Rest in the Arms of Love

[This message is from "Lady Whale", a member of the Whale Collective. She is the one who guided KGH to the Crystal City for the council meeting.] We, the Whales, are in the process of shifting in harmony with the great heart of Gaia, Mother Earth. She is shifting into a higher frequency, shaking and stretching into her new shape, expanding and growing. Just breathe in the knowingness that this is for all who are upon her. We are helping to keep an opening for you to be a conduit for the love of All That Is.

We have much to share as you feel our love for all of humanity. There are many shifts approaching. We want you to understand the wisdom in this, as they are of a grand nature. The earth is holding a place for you to grow into the new geometric patterns of life. Know that this is the template of creation, giving your heart and mind a place to focus and hold the new hologram that will be the new template for your bodies. Be in your heart and sing your love for Gaia, the mother of our bodies. We are expecting and holding much in her awakening as she allows us to be her breath.[14] Be a part of this breath with us, the Whales, in the heart of remembering. Be in your heart and allow the love of All That Is to flow through you.

Help us bring in and hold the new patterns that are for the expansion of Self, in the heart of all creation. Be gentle in your touch and in your judging of self. Be gentle with your holding of these energies. This allows them to move into you and expand all around, to be available for others to feel and open to. Do not worry, just be and breathe your love to all.

Be open to possibilities of love flowing to you from unexpected places. There are many who are expressing love to you and all humanity. The love that is flowing into this planet is immense and beyond the ability of the human mind to comprehend. Allow us to help guide you and allow

[14] *Breath Keepers:* The Whales are the Breath Keepers of our planet (and most likely, many more worlds). With their physical conscious breathing they create balance in our world and recycle the life force in the atmosphere of Gaia. The breath is a metaphor for the Grand Cycle of Loving.

this love to fill your heart. We are in joy that all is being expressed in the light of loving each other. This grand love is about to explode in the hearts of all. We are teaching you to see and hear and feel this love that is flowing into our part of the galaxy. Be in your heart as these energies expand. In an instant all will be love. Fill your hearts with the love of loving each other. Keep being love. Know that in this expansion all are welcome. We are holding the *generator of this breath of loving*.[15] We are loving you and all that are part of this love expressed in the heart of loving.

Be with us and feel our breath as it opens the door for love to fill you. You can be more than this template you are in now, more than you ever imagined in your mind. Be with us in the breath of All That Is and feel the beginning of this expansion. It will be a new way of expressing. Be in the breath, in the now that is breath. Feel the love that is flowing in and all around you. You are welcoming your Self to be love expressed as you open to the heart of All That Is. Keep yourself in

---

[15] *Generator of the breath of loving:* A sphere of spinning, pulsing, bluish white light embodying the image the earth in the center of the gathering in the Crystal City. All of the participants breathe the light they carry from their homes through their hearts, beaming rays that culminate in the center of the sphere. This sphere represents the heart of Gaia.

the breath of all creation. Being in your heart is how we are becoming each other, allowing you to be us, the Whales, in the heart of our love for you, the Humans.[16]

The last of the old is playing out in a desperate act of survival. But this too, is love. Just be loving and everyone will find love in their own way and time. Do not dwell in fear, do not teach fear. Be the light of love. Trust in your Selves, in your heart, in the loving of all.

We all are embarking on a new journey. As we expand our awareness we learn to be the love of All That Is in every breath. In every now we are love expressed. Be this love and allow freedom to all who are part of this, who are playing their parts, fulfilling their agreements in the grand play of Self, learning and expressing who/what they are being called to be. Even if you are not in agreement with another being's perspective, still allow them to be and find their way to the love that awaits them. By holding love in your core and filling your breath with love expressed, it is there for others to find. This will lead them to their own heart, into the cycle of finding, holding and expressing love, bringing them ever closer to

---

[16] I am you, and you are me, in the heart of All That Is. Namaste.

remembering that they are the breath of All That Is.

I, Lady Whale, am here as a friend, as a guide for you to be a part of our circle. We are excited that you are wanting to be a part of what we are sharing. We are gifting you with more than we are. We are bringing you to a new plateau of knowing. The foundation has been laid. You are in our hearts. We are loving you. We are helping you to be more than even you have dreamed of, in the expression you have been from your first breath.

Be open to what we are saying to you. Be in the empowerment of Self. Expand as you hear us. With every breath, expand just a bit more. Be in the allowing of your true expression as love; expand into this reality. You can be more than you are allowing. Just trust yourself. Trust us, the Whales, and take the steps that will allow you to open to your true Self. Feel our love as we sing to you. You are key to this plan. We are loving you and nurturing you to becoming your true Self expressed in this lifetime. Embrace the love of All That Is. Keep loving yourself and know that you can do and be more than your ego is allowing you to see.

Sing with us and we can guide you to this. This is why we have invited you to be with us here in the Crystal City of Light and Hope, the Crystal City of Ever Expanding Love, the place where you are opened and nurtured into finding Self, to becoming Self, in our loving arms.

We are the Whales in you.

Chapter 11

Weaving the Web

Today is a day of resting in each other arms, feeling the love we have for each other and our connection to All That Is. Be in your heart this day and feel the breath of life as it circles around you. Be in your heart, knowing that we are here with you. Just be and let be. Touch all with the love of your song. Fill yourself with light from Source and breathe in love from the Earth.

Find a place of peace in your heart and be open to what is coming in as love from the many beings that are here as part of this opening to the expansion of all. Just open and allow love, letting it connect and intertwine you in the web. Be and share the power of loving. Feel how this brings joy and uplifts you in your heart, connecting you to the core of Self. Let this loving web be your support. Know you are always interconnecting with all who are becoming this light of loving. If you look closer you will see that all beings are connected in this love. Just see the pure light that is in every heart and know that even if it appears that they are not loving, they are truly beings of love. Hold a space for them and shine the beacon of loving that allows them the choice to step into the web of loving that connects and supports us all, feeding us in our creation, with the love of All That Is.

Being in your core, in the center of the vortex, in that calm place, allows these pulses of love to fill you and helps you understand and feel you are not alone and are loved by so many. You cannot even comprehend the truth of this reality with your mind, but this is truth. Understand that seeing this in your mind's eye anchors the loving grid into you and into the earth, creating a flow of loving energy that feeds us and give us a deeper knowingness that we all are Love.

We are the Whales in you, the Council of Seven and all the Beings that are loving you from the Heart of All That Is.

[KGH: I see this huge web that gives us all a place to be connected. As we sing this song of loving, the strings of the web vibrate and gift our love to the many Selves and remind us that we are not alone, that we are loved and give love, constantly. We are always touching each other and this is the connection we share with all who open to love from Source. We know this as we shift our perspective and listen deeply in our hearts. Feel the songs of loving from all who are in this web. They are singing, listening and sharing, with all that they are, with all that we are, loving all, being all and connecting us with the Love of Source. We are weaving this web, together as one heart.]

About the Authors

Keith Grey Hale is the president and co-founder of Gray Whale Wisdom, Inc. He has served as a naturalist with the Santa Barbara Channel Island National Marine Sanctuary providing educational information to passengers on Santa Barbara Channel whale watching trips. He has also served as a docent and educator at the Santa Barbara Natural History Museum Ty Warner Sea Center, additionally volunteering for outreach programs in our local schools, sharing information and appreciation for cetaceans and all life in our oceans. "Throughout my life I have been involved with the ocean whether boating, fishing, surfing, or scuba diving. I feel more at home in the water than on land." Keith is also an accomplished jewelry artist and teaches silversmithing at the local adult education center.

Carolyn M. Gorman is a board officer and co-founder and of Gray Whale Wisdom, Inc. She brings her passion for writing poetry and creative prose to the process of writing and editing inspirational works of literature. Spirit has been speaking to and through her since childhood and been a driving force in her personal and vocational journey through life.

Gray Whale Wisdom, Inc. is a nonprofit organization focused on Cetacean Education, developing enriching programs and materials to share the beauty, grace and intelligence of whales and dolphins. Through exploration of the broader concepts of consciousness, in regards to cetaceans in particular, we gain a deeper understanding of the world in which we all live. The more aware and educated we are about the beings with whom we share our planet, the better prepared we will be to make conscious choices every day in all aspects of our lives. Through education and inspiration Gray Whale Wisdom strives to promote a greater appreciation for the interconnection of all life and a sense of stewardship toward our planet Earth. We have much to learn from these denizens of the sea and they are anxious to teach us!

www.graywhalewisdom.com

Made in the USA
Charleston, SC
30 September 2015